Responding with COMPASSION

Navigating CHALLENGING BEHAVIORS in SPECIAL NEEDS Ministry

by Jennifer McNally

Responding with Compassion
Print: ISBN 978-1-946237-14-9
Kindle: ISBN 978-1-946237-15-6
EPUB: ISBN 978-1-946237-16-3

Author: Jennifer McNally
Collaborators: Cameryn Bartschi and Carrie Jones
Contributing Editors: Ali Howard and Mike Dobes
Editor in Chief: Eric Jones

Printed in the United States of America.

Produced by The Denzel Agency (www.denzel.org)
Cover and Interior Design: Rob Williams

For information or to order additional print copies of this and other resources contact:

Joni and Friends International Disability Center
P.O. Box 3333, Agoura Hills, California 91376-3333
Email: churchrelations@joniandfriends.org
Phone: 818-707-5664

Kindle version available at www.irresistiblechurch.org

CONTENTS

PART I

Responding with Compassion

Psalm 139:14 says, "I praise you because I am fearfully and wonderfully made." God created every single one of us for a reason, for a purpose. He made us all unique and special. His desire is for us to praise and serve him using the gifts and talents he has given to us. As believers, we are called to be the hands and feet of Jesus; we are called to help all his people feel loved. When we create a church environment where people of all abilities are loved and made to feel welcome, we are acting as the hands and feet of Jesus. When you reach out to families affected by disability, you are honoring Christ. When you begin a disability ministry in your church, you are reflecting God's love in your community, and you are engaged in becoming an Irresistible Church. An Irresistible Church is "an authentic community built on the hope of Christ that compels people affected by disability to fully belong." When your disability ministry begins to grow and form, I believe your church will mature and you will be blessed. Luke 14:13-14a tells us, "But when you give a banquet, invite the poor, the crippled, the lame, and the blind, and you will be blessed."

If you are reading this book, you may already have a ministry geared toward meeting the needs of families affected by disability. Others of you may just be taking the first steps to starting one. In her book titled *Special Needs Ministry*, Pat Verbal says that special needs ministries are aimed at meeting the spiritual needs of those who have disabilities. A special needs ministry (or disability ministry) reaches out to children and adults with disabilities as well as their families. In many cases, friends who have disabilities can benefit the most from inclusion with their peers. While Jesus was on Earth, he spent time with people who had disabilities. He included everyone he encountered. We can share this same love with others and use the model that Jesus set for us by having relationships with people impacted by disabilities and by welcoming them into our churches. Although it may, forming a disability ministry does not necessarily mean starting a new program from the ground up. It's about having an open heart, an open mind, and a willingness to do things a little bit differently. All people are invited to participate in God's Church, so in the following pages, I hope to give you some tools and tips on helping our friends with disabilities fully belong. When you venture into the world of disability ministry, I have confidence that God will equip you with the ability to welcome everyone and allow them to feel loved.

Special needs are disabilities that keep individuals from progressing at a normal pace (Verbal, 2004). Discipling our friends with special needs can sometimes require intentional planning, teaching, and training. Disabilities you may see in your church could include but are not limited to physical disabilities, hearing impairments, visual disabilities, learning disabilities, and intellectual impairments. Every person has a unique style of learning. Getting to know each individual in your class and supporting them with intentional planning can help you meet the needs of every friend in your ministry. If you do create (or already have) a special needs ministry, there is a chance that some of your friends may have short attention spans, impulsive behaviors, trouble with motor skills, mood changes, problems with social interaction, and challenging behavior. Fortunately, intentional planning can help you reach everyone in your ministry, regardless of their ability level. To assist you in effectively reaching each friend in your ministry, it can be helpful to understand their disabilities. But beyond that, it can also be helpful if you become familiar with proactive strategies that will help everyone positively engage in your ministry. In the following pages, we will take a closer look at behavior as communication as well as at a variety of practical, proactive approaches that can help your ministry programs run smoothly and hopefully allow you the ability to teach effectively. These approaches can be useful when teaching Sunday school, in holding respite events, for inclusive community festivals, or even for engaging in a newfound friendship. With this open mind, open heart, and the ability to see things a little differently, you are well on the path to becoming an Irresistible Church. An

This symbol indicates that there are supplemental resources that correspond with this topic at http://irresistiblechurch.org/library/

Irresistible Church allows all people to feel a sense of welcoming and belonging with the ability to worship and serve together. An Irresistible Church is about building relationships and friendships in an inclusive environment, just like Jesus showed us through his life on Earth. Learning more about behavior as communication and proactive behavioral strategies can help you to become more irresistible to families affected by disability.

There may be times when a friend engages in disruptive or challenging behaviors, making it difficult for them to integrate into the life of the church. We want all our friends to feel welcome at church, even if it appears that certain behaviors are preventing them from engaging. I have heard stories of churches not knowing how to help when difficult behaviors are involved. These churches sometimes ask parents to keep their child with them during worship or to sit outside with them in the hallway. This kind of response can be incredibly discouraging to parents who are trying to find a church where they are loved, included, and welcomed. I can't help but wonder if this sometimes happens because the leaders are not sure where to start or how they can help. It can certainly be overwhelming for a church teacher or volunteer if they have an individual in their class who is exhibiting challenging behaviors. These leaders may try a few techniques they know, but in the end, they struggle to understand what their friend is communicating. They want to do what is best for everyone involved but cannot figure out what their friend is trying to say, and so they ask the parents or caregivers to take the individual from the room to minimize distractions for others. It is our role to teach *all people* when they come to our churches. Matthew 28:19 tells us to "Go therefore and make disciples of all nations, baptizing them in the name of the Father and of the Son and of the Holy Spirit." The important word in this verse is "all." My hope is that the information in this book can help you learn how to interpret the challenging behaviors of your friends and to implement proactive strategies so that we can all join in worship and learning together.

PART II

Behavior as Communication

"Change the way you see things and the things you see will change."
—ANONYMOUS

All behavior is communication in some form or fashion. When you view behavior in this way, it can give you a new level of patience and understanding. Becoming familiar with the idea that all behaviors are simply a way to communicate can help your class run more smoothly and effectively.

We all communicate through our behaviors. A toddler fusses when tired. An adult lets out a sigh when exasperated. A child cries because she is afraid of the dark. A student knocks over a chair because his teacher does not see him raising his hand. A teenager rolls her eyes because her mother will not let her have the car.

Many times, our friends affected by disability may not have the words to communicate what they need, so they use other strategies to express their desires. Imagine how hard it would be to have a strong need or desire and not be able to communicate or express it to anyone. If you must rely on others to meet your needs, the inability to express yourself would be incredibly frustrating. Many times, our friends may be seen as "bad," acting out, or in need of punishment. When we see our friends exhibiting challenging behaviors in church or in public, we ought to give them grace. They may be unable to communicate and are simply trying to get their needs across. They may be completely overstimulated, scared, or confused. Instead of staring or quickly walking by, we should see if they need help or if there is anything we can do. When Jesus was on Earth, he did not ignore people with disabilities; instead, he spent time with them. He became their friend and walked alongside them. When we see a friend who is upset or appears to be acting out, we should assume that they are more than likely trying to find a way to communicate with their parent, caregiver, teacher, or some other person. When individuals impacted by disability come to church, it would be helpful to understand what they are trying to say. By taking time to observe and understand behavior as communication, we are acting as the hands and feet of Jesus.

The purpose of this book is not to provide an exhaustive explanation of behavioral therapy. However, to begin understanding what a behavior might be communicating, it is helpful to understand what clinical behavioral specialists call the four categories or functions of behavior. The acronym SEAT can be used as a way to remember these functions.

S—Sensory. Any behavior in this category communicates a preferred sensory experience. Through their behavior, your friend is expressing a desire for sensory input (jumping, feeling a texture, being wrapped in a weighted blanket, etc.).

E—Escape. This category covers behavior that communicates a desire to get away from someone or something. Perhaps your friend is uncomfortable with the noise level of a large group or is fearful of engaging in certain activities. Their behavior will communicate their desire to *not* participate in these environments or activities.

A—Attention. Behavior in this category communicates that your friend is trying to capture the attention of someone. In the same way that we often precede a request with someone's name ("John, will you help me carry this?"), our friends may use their behavior to grab our attention and communicate their desires to us.

T—Tangibles. This category of behavior communicates a desire for access to a preferred item or activity. We all have activities or items that we love and enjoy doing. Our friends may use their behavior to express their desire to engage with something they like.

Understanding behavior in light of these four functions can help us understand what someone with challenging behavior might be trying to communicate. The following suggestions can also be helpful as you seek to gain further understanding of your friends' behaviors.

1. *Communicate with parents and caregivers.* Many individuals with challenging behaviors work regularly with behavioral therapists and have behavioral strategies already in place at school or at home. Asking your friends' parents and caregivers how they approach disruptive behaviors will give you great insight into how to reinforce the established strategies rather than creating new ones. This consistency can go a long way in

preventing challenging behavior. Parents and caregivers can also help educate you on particular behaviors and what your friend is trying to say when engaging in that behavior.

2. *Observe patterns.* As you interact with the individuals in your ministry, you may be able to identify certain patterns that act as triggers for challenging behaviors. The proactive strategies in the following section will help to avoid many disruptive behaviors, but sometimes a closer look is needed. Carefully observing what happens before and after your friends' behaviors may help you gain clarity on what they are communicating.
3. *Embrace and teach acceptance.* While we certainly want to minimize challenging behaviors within our ministries, part of loving our friends with disabilities is accepting the noises they make or the actions they exhibit. I encourage you to meet your friends where they are and love them for who they are, allowing them to truly be part of the church family. As you get to know your friends and learn to understand their behaviors, you will begin to identify behaviors that need to be addressed because of their disruptive

> nature. But you will also begin to see behaviors that can be accepted and enjoyed, such as singing loudly, shouting in excitement or happiness, clapping, or repeating what someone says. While some of these behaviors are foreign to us or the peers in our ministries, they are not challenging or in need of correction. Rather, it is our perception and heart that should be open to embracing the unique communication styles of our friends.

If you are interested in learning more about the functions of behavior and the clinical side of behavioral therapy, I encourage you to connect with a local Board Certified Behavioral Analyst. Individuals trained in this area of specialty can provide a wealth of information on understanding behaviors.

For the purpose of leading your ministry though, you do not need to be a behavioral specialist. With the following proactive strategies and by the grace of God, you should be able to positively navigate most of the challenging behaviors that may arise in your ministry.

PART III

Proactive Strategies

"Every student can learn,
just not on the same day, or in the same way."
—George Evans

As a former special education teacher and buddy in a disability ministry program, I have found that it is much easier to be proactive than reactive. It is easier to set up the environment in a way that prevents challenging behaviors from occurring than it is to put a corrective plan in place after a behavior presents itself. It is easier to keep your friend engaged in activities and lessons, and thus not giving him a chance to lose interest, than it is to catch him halfway down the hall. It is easier to keep materials we are not using out of reach than it is to repeatedly tell a friend to not touch. It is easier to transition a group of people to a new activity if the leader is enthusiastic and the activity enticing than it is to repeatedly ask people to join you at the table.

I learned through observation, reflection, and experience that it is much easier, more engaging, and more beneficial for everyone involved if you put thought into how you understand behaviors, arrange your schedule, and set up your lesson plan. When you are intentional with your planning and setup, it can have a significant, positive impact on the behaviors of the individuals with whom you are working. We'll take a closer look at doing this practically through positive reinforcement, modifying the ministry environment, and modifying lesson plans.

For the sake of this book, I am going to use the word "classroom" to describe all the places you may be engaged in ministry. You may call your Sunday school class a class, a room, or something completely different. You may call it a Life or Connection Group, Young Seekers, or the Teen Zone. You may even be engaging in ministry at a park, a camp, or with a sports team. Ministry can happen at any of these places and is unique to each church. When you see the word "classroom," please remember that ministry can take place within any of these contexts.

Before we dive into the details of these proactive strategies, I would like to suggest that the first thing we should do when a problem arises in our ministries (or even when things are going well) is pray. We should pray for our disability ministry programs and for the friends who participate in our programs. We should pray that our ministries will reach new families and that volunteers will continue to step up to the job. We should ask God to fill us with his love, kindness, and gentleness. The love that you pour out to these individuals may be just what they need. Proverbs 31:26 tells us, "She opens her mouth with wisdom, and the teaching of kindness is on her tongue." The Bible instructs and encourages us to be the teachers that lead our friends on a path of knowing their Savior and Lord.

a. *POSITIVE REINFORCEMENT*

Behavior is an observable, learned response. Reinforcement can encourage either appropriate or challenging behavior. In my classroom, it has always been my goal to use reinforcement to help increase the chances that an appropriate and desired behavior will occur more often in the future. Positive reinforcement means that something motivating is presented to your friend after the behavior occurs, encouraging them to continue doing that behavior.

Allow me to share an example of positive reinforcement: a young girl has been working on learning how to walk in line. When you see your friend walking in line, you say to her, "I love how you are walking in line today. Great job!" This positive reinforcement will hopefully help this behavior occur more often in the future. When using positive reinforcement, it is most helpful if you offer the praise right when the appropriate behavior occurs.

When using positive reinforcement with your friends to increase and encourage desired behaviors, it is helpful to know what is motivating to each friend in your ministry. All of us have different likes and dislikes, and it can make a difference in the behaviors displayed in your classroom if you get to know these preferences. If you provide reinforcement that is not motivating to your friend, it will not help the desired behavior continue. You can easily gain this information from the parent or caregiver as they will know what works well at home or at school. You may even ask parents and caregivers to complete a short form about their loved one that helps you get to know them better. Some things that can motivate and reinforce good behavior include praise, a sticker, or getting to assist the Sunday school teacher or leader with the next activity. As you get to know your friends, you may find that some individuals work well with a lot of positive reinforcement while others do not need as much. It can also be helpful to remember that your friends' preferences may change over time, causing you to reevaluate what positive reinforcements you use. What works well now may not work as well in the future.

b. *MODIFYING THE CLASSROOM ENVIRONMENT*

Identifying the cause of challenging behaviors can be very beneficial for everyone in the classroom. There may be times when finding out the cause prompts you to make modifications. Often, there are small, simple changes you can make to help prevent challenging behaviors from occurring. Students benefit from an environment that is organized and comfortable. By putting a little extra thought into how you set up your environment and execute your classroom management, you can avoid many behavioral challenges. When you consider setting up or modifying your environment, you may want to consider the following things:

- Classroom rules
- Classroom design
    - Sensory space
- Scheduling and pacing
- Modeling
- Transitions
- Using visuals
- Offering choices
- Leader responses
    - Encouragement
    - Call and response
- Peer modeling
- Using volunteers and buddies

Considering these topics when planning or adapting your classroom can make a difference that will help our friends affected by disability learn about the love of Jesus Christ. We'll take a look at each of these topics in more detail in the following pages.

Classroom Rules

If we lived our lives without rules, we would live in chaos. If no one followed traffic rules, driving would be incredibly difficult. Imagine if no one followed the speed limit, stopped at stop signs, stopped at red lights, or stayed in the correct traffic lane. If we did not have these traffic rules, we would not know what was expected of us or how to drive on the roads. Having traffic rules lets us know how to drive, what to do, and what is expected of us. They help keep us safe on the roads and provide structure for driving.

Setting up rules for your classroom can be just as helpful. Communicating clear expectations for your ministry helps everyone know what is expected of them and allows for fewer distractions, which can help your friends stay focused on the lesson. You may want to post the rules where everyone can see them. You might choose to frequently visit the rules to reinforce appropriate behaviors. It can be helpful if rules are written as a positive statement--what your friends *should* be doing, rather than what they *should not* be doing. Rules that are focused and clear tend to be easier to follow. Having a few rules that cover the behaviors you want to see will set your Sunday school class or ministry group up for the most success. If you have too many rules, your friends will likely become overwhelmed and not be able to remember them. Three to five rules is a good guide to use. When creating your rules, keep in mind the age of your friends. An example of five rules for a class of younger students is as follows:

CLASSROOM RULES:

1. Looking eyes
2. Listening ears
3. Quiet mouth
4. Helping hands
5. Walking feet

Next to each rule, you could have a picture so that children who are not readers can visually "read" the rule. It is helpful if you explain to your friends what each rule means and give them examples to promote further understanding. "Looking eyes" means that the children are looking either at the speaker or at the activity they are working on. "Listening ears" means they are listening to what the speaker is saying. "Quiet mouth" means that the students are not talking out of turn. "Helping hands" means that students are using gentle touches with friends or peers in the class. "Walking feet" means just as it says: that the children should be walking rather than running. A way to continue reinforcing the rules is to have the class read them with you or repeat them after you.

A sample for friends who are older could look something like this:

MINISTRY GUIDELINES:

1. Respect everyone
2. Listen to your leaders
3. Make wise choices

You could explain what respect means and what it looks like to show respect. You might plan lessons on following leaders or on wisdom. These lessons could be something that you re-visit again and again. There are many verses in the Bible that you could use to teach the rules listed above. You could use 1 Corinthians 16:14; 1 Peter 1:22; Hebrews 13:17; 1 Thessalonians 5:12-13; Proverbs 19:20; or James 1:5.

It can also be a great idea to use pictures of your friends to represent each rule. You could take pictures of them "doing" the rules and post them on a poster board for all to see. Taking pictures of your friends acting out what the rules mean builds confidence and self-esteem while also reinforcing the rules. You could consider choosing a friend who does not always follow the rules to be on your Sunday school classroom poster. In doing so, you reinforce their appropriate behavior. You could also catch a friend doing something "good" (exhibiting one of the rules) and ask if you can photograph him or her portraying that rule. For many of our friends who have behavioral challenges, it can mean a lot to them to be portrayed in such a positive way.

Classroom Design

We all love a cozy home, a comforting bedroom, a soothing office. If my office is a mess, I feel like I cannot concentrate. At home, if my children cannot find their backpacks or other belongings, things can quickly get chaotic. Some of you may keep your cars sparkling clean or keep a very tidy garage. Just like you and I enjoy welcoming and organized environments, our friends with disabilities generally do best in this type of environment as well. When we create a welcoming classroom environment, we increase each friend's ability to learn and hear the gospel.

Creating a welcoming classroom typically means keeping it clean and tidy, elements that help most everyone improve their focus. Limiting clutter can especially help our friends with autism and ADHD. Creating a welcoming environment also includes keeping noise to a minimum, which can help children with a visual or learning impairment. It means remaining calm on the outside even if you do not feel it on the inside. A welcoming environment involves lots of smiling and possibly some singing. It means being colorful and bright but not overwhelming. It also means organizing your furniture in a way that is visually appealing. If you have tables, line them up in neat rows and push the chairs under the tables. If any of your friends have wheelchairs or walkers, you will want to leave space for them at the table as well. In the Irresistible Church book titled *Pathways to Belonging*, you will find some great questions to ask yourself regarding environments, including, "Do wheelchair users have room to move and participate fully?" or "Is the room attractive and inviting but not too overwhelming for students with sensory sensitivity?" (p 22). Having a classroom with ample space can help everyone move around more freely. If you are leading a ministry that serves younger children, hanging artwork at the eye level of the students in the class is also good to do if you are able. Children love to see their artwork on display and it makes the room colorful and cozy. When you hang artwork or other visuals on the walls, do so in a way that is orderly and not overwhelming as too much clutter can be distracting for children with autism or ADHD.

In *Pathways to Belonging*, it is also noted that making minor classroom adaptions can be extremely helpful. One such adaptation can be having a sensory space. If you do not have the room for a dedicated sensory space, you can make a sensory bag or box. These calming objects or areas can make a critical difference for a friend who is overstimulated. You can let your friend spend a few minutes in the sensory area and then invite him or her back to the group once he or she is calm again. For a friend who struggles with sensory overload, it may even be a good idea to plan scheduled sensory breaks throughout your time together as a proactive strategy to help them feel calm and comfortable.

Scheduling and Pacing

"Schedules present the abstract concept of time in a concrete, visual form."[1] This is an important component of life for most people. I recently misplaced my calendar. I still use a paper-and-pencil type notebook to schedule my professional and personal schedule. This schedule helps me balance the demands of a full-time job, a husband, two young children, and a few animals. Misplacing my calendar caused feelings of stress, anxiety, helplessness, and a loss of control. I explained to my co-workers what I had done, inquiring if they had seen it anywhere, and asking them to help me remember upcoming events. I searched my house, and re-traced my steps. I felt lost and truly did not know what to do. I became reliant on others for help until I finally remembered taking it into a grocery store with me, as I had written my grocery list in it. I eventually recovered my calendar, and my life resumed its normal rhythms. For others of you, you may experience a similar feeling if you misplace your cellphone or even your wallet. Either way, that "lost" feeling is not a pleasant experience.

The unsettling experience I just described is very similar to what someone with autism may feel on a daily basis if visual supports and schedules are not in place. They may feel lost and anxious. They may not understand what is expected of them and will become dependent on others to help them move from one activity to the next. They may eventually shut down, just like I wanted to do when I misplaced my calendar. Having a clear schedule can increase feelings of security for our friends and can help them to feel in control. Our friends, as well as many others in our churches, could benefit from the comfort and security of using a visual schedule.

"A visual schedule communicates the sequence of upcoming activities or events through the use of objects, photographs, icons, words or a combination of tangible supports."[2] A schedule provides structure and builds trust among the leaders and participants in your ministry. In preschool, kindergarten, or other classes in your church where you have an individual who is not reading, you should have clear and easily understood pictures for your schedule. It is not uncommon to see challenging behaviors decrease when a schedule is clearly communicated. Having a posted, visual schedule helps individuals better understand transitions and expectations. A consistent and clear schedule for your ministry or church builds relationships between leaders, volunteers, and parents. It also helps the parents or caregivers know what is happening during your ministry time with their loved one. For the leaders and volunteers in the room, it can help them stay on task and plan each lesson intentionally.

A schedule should be posted where everyone can easily see it. If you have young children in your ministry, try to hang the schedule at their eye level. Posting the schedule with Velcro or magnet strips allows you to change the pictures as needed. The schedule should allow for some flexibility as there may be changes that are not in your control, for example, getting together with another class to watch a video or changing your recess time because it is raining. These changes could alter the order of your schedule completely. When you need to make changes to your schedule, it can be helpful to give your friends as much of a heads-up as possible. At the beginning of your time together, you can have the changes prepared and explain how the day is going to go. This can help alleviate the anxiety that may come from having changes in the regular schedule.

I have had great success including a balanced variety of activities in the schedule and would encourage you to consider doing the same. You could include active and quiet activities, large-group and small-group, as well as individual-directed (the individuals get to choose the activity) and leader-directed (the leader is in charge of choosing the activity). This variety can help your time together flow smoothly. For example, you could allow everyone to quietly work on an art project, and then have large-group music time. Your friends could choose the next activity, and then the leader chooses what table everyone goes to for small-group time. Having this kind of variety in your schedule gives your friends a sense of control but also lets them know who the leader is and who is in charge during your ministry time. Having variety in your schedule can also help keep your friends engaged.

Another component to consider when creating your schedule is pacing. Pacing, in this case, refers to the amount of time you give to each activity in your schedule. You should take into consideration the attention span of your friends when setting your schedule, even if you only share an hour together on Sunday mornings. If some of your activities go too long, you will lose the attention of your friends. If it is too quick, your friends may get frustrated if they do not have time to complete an activity. If your friends get bored with an activity that is going on for too long, you may see difficult behaviors begin to arise. If you start to recognize this happening in your ministry, you might consider shortening the time for the current activity and switching to the next one.

Imagine you are a family impacted by disability looking for a new church. Your child uses a picture schedule at school five days a week with great success, and you also implement this system at home to provide consistency and structure. Now, imagine walking into your child's new Sunday school room and seeing a visual schedule posted on the wall. Imagine the relief and feeling of belonging this simple thing would provide for your entire family. What a wonderful experience and first visit this church would be providing for your family. This would truly make the church look irresistible to you and your family.

Modeling

"With an upright heart he shepherded them and guided them with his skillful hand" (Psalm 78:72). As teachers and ministry leaders, we become like shepherds to our sheep, just as our Heavenly Father is to us. He guides us, leads us, and teaches us. And just as he always sets a good example for us, we too must set good examples for the individuals under our leadership. This means being a good model and good example. I have often cringed as a ministry leader or teacher tells their class, "Don't sit on the table," while sitting on the table themselves. The actions and words of this teacher are contradictory, leaving their friends confused. As a leader, you should tell *and show* your friends what you expect, modeling these expectations with your own behavior. Another example of poor modeling behavior would be leaders and volunteers who chat in the back of the room while expecting their friends to work on a project without talking. Volunteers chatting with one another while the teacher is trying to teach is also very distracting for everyone and sends mixed signals. A good rule of thumb is to act how you want your class to act, do what you want your class to do. In doing so, you will be a good model for your class.

Modeling can also refer to showing your friends what you are expecting them to do. If you would like them to place their musical instruments in a bin, it is much more effective if you do this motion as you explain the instructions rather than just telling them to do it. So, the teacher giving the instructions would take their instrument and actually walk over to the bin to visually show the class where they should place their instrument. When you model an action or activity for your group, it is typically helpful to let your actions do most of the communication, keeping your words to a minimum. Your actions should do the talking for you.

Transitions

Transitioning refers to the time period that exists between learning activities. Transitions can take time away from your lesson and can also be a potential opportunity for challenging behaviors to take place. Most ministries have limited time together each week, time that you likely want for intentional teaching and discipleship. It is not unusual for a ministry to get bogged down with transitions, especially if you have a large group. Transitions are a prime time for your friends to become distracted, potentially leading to challenging behaviors and frustration for leaders. When your transitions are quick and seamless, learning can continue, and your carefully thought-through schedule can remain smooth and on track. When planning for smooth transitions, you should decide what type of signal you would like to use. A few suggestions might include a timer with an alarm sound, a song, or a chant. This signal will alert your friends to the time so that they can easily see how much time is left for a particular activity. I personally find it helpful to use different signals between different activities. If you have access to a smart board, iPhone, or iPad, there are many apps for visual countdown timers. As an example, when I was a full-time teacher, I liked to use a lunch song when it was lunchtime, a timer with an alarm when it was time to clean up, and a line-up chant when it was time to line up.

Allow me to share a few tips for easy transitions:

1. Announce that a transition is about to take place—for example, "In 2 minutes, we are going to clean up our snacks and move to our seats for our Bible lesson. So, when you hear the clean-up bell (song, timer, etc.), I would like you to begin cleaning up."
2. Signal the transition with a cue—a song, a bell, a video, etc. There are some great clean-up videos online; or you can sing a song or say a rhyme, or simply use a bell.
3. Assist your friends with cleaning up.
4. Have a teacher or volunteer stay with anyone who needs a little extra time to transition.
5. Have the teacher or leader model what to do or where to go next. If you are going to the circle area for story time, move over to the circle area and have a seat. Sing a song or play a short game with the individuals who have moved to the circle already. Try to make it exciting and engaging for your friends so that they will want to move over to the new activity quickly.

One Sunday, while getting a class of young children to the carpet for a Bible lesson, I played "Ring Around the Rosy" as there were a few kids who were reluctant to come. Involving the class in this fun activity enticed the others to quickly join us and we had fun while doing it. Intentionally setting up transitions to be fun, quick, and seamless will save you time, allowing you to spend more time focused on sharing the gospel lesson and activity.

Using Visuals

Imagine you are visiting France. It is time for dinner, and you are starving. You may know a few words in French, but you cannot read French at all. You approach a restaurant to review the menu, but everything is written in French. Your stomach is growling as you try to make sense out of the words on the menu—an extremely challenging task. You decide to try a different restaurant. As you review their menu, you notice there are pictures beside the words. Suddenly, ordering becomes much easier! You breathe a sigh of relief knowing your hunger pangs will soon subside. This example shows us how important visual supports are to us in our everyday lives.

Everyone falls into one (or a combination) of four categories of learning—auditory, which is learning by listening; visual, which is learning by seeing; tactile, which is learning through hands-on experiences;

and experiential, which is learning through being immersed in the story or activity. As I mentioned in the section on scheduling, using visuals in a ministry setting is very important for individuals with disabilities. Visual supports can help them increase their focus, decrease anxiety, express their thoughts, and establish routine, structure, and sequence for your time together.

Visual supports can be used in many different ways. You could take screen shots, use clip art, or draw pictures on a whiteboard when going over the lesson or activity. Using pictures to label where things go in the classroom can help create independence and can also help your room stay organized, neat, and welcoming. You can label things like supply bins or bookshelves. I have also had a lot of success using large STOP signs with children who tend to elope (run). I attach (using tape or Velcro) the STOP sign to a door, and it helps communicate to that child that they are to stop and not run out the door. You can also use the STOP sign if you do not want your friends to open a certain cabinet or closet. As with all visual aids, it can be helpful if you explain what they mean to your friends to ensure they understand what is expected. There are many websites online with free visuals.

Visuals can also be beneficial in helping to set boundaries, especially with younger children who tend to need more help in this area. For example, you could use carpet squares during large-group times. These carpet squares can help your young friends keep their hands and feet to themselves. It can also help reduce distractions and increase focus. If you cannot find carpet squares, you could also use seat cushions or round bath mats. You could also use masking tape to create clear boundaries at shared tables or even on the floor when lining up.

Offering Choices

We all like to have choices throughout our day. It is part of our human nature. We like to be in control, and we usually know what we want. We go to lunch at a restaurant and we are presented with many options to choose from. We know if we want our coffee or tea with sugar and cream, and we have dozens of options when buying bread at the grocery store. We enjoy the freedom and independence that these choices bring us. Offering choices to our friends also builds self-esteem. It helps them accept responsibility and allows them to feel like they have some control. It can also help reduce conflict between your friends and ministry leaders.

When you present your friend with options to choose from, keep in mind that offering a limited number of choices will allow them independence without overwhelming them. I suggest providing two options that are already desirable for the teacher or caregiver. Offering choices within activities can be a great way of providing an opportunity to make a choice. For example, during an art activity you could offer your friend the choice of using stickers or stamps. During snack time, they can choose one banana or one pack of crackers. As you plan your ministry time, think about how you can incorporate choices for your friends.

Leader Responses

The way a leader or volunteer responds to challenging behaviors can also increase or decrease that behavior. If an individual in your ministry yells at one of the volunteers and the volunteer yells back, that is likely the start of a downward spiral. On the other hand, if one of your friends yells at the teacher and the teacher looks her in the eyes and speaks to her in a soft voice, that would probably help to calm your friend down. Leaders in your ministry should always strive to show compassion and gentleness to individuals who are exhibiting challenging behaviors. Most times, the individual exhibiting the behavior is just trying to communicate their wants or needs to others.

I love the Japanese proverb that says, "One who smiles rather than rages is always the stronger." Whenever the class or an individual becomes loud, it is natural to want to speak louder so that they can hear you. But have you ever tried getting quiet in these loud moments? An amazing thing can happen! Often, your friends and others in the room will get quiet so they can hear what you are saying! This lowers the stress level of the entire room and allows you to continue giving instruction.

Sometimes, an individual will behave a certain way to get a response from his or her teacher. The teacher's reaction to that behavior could encourage the individual to continue doing that behavior. For example, if the teacher takes a young friend to the side and gives them extra (disciplinary) attention for a disruptive behavior, the child may continue engaging in that behavior to receive the extra attention. A positive way to prevent this is to catch that individual doing something good. When you point out your friend doing something good, you are giving attention to your friend and to their appropriate behavior, which will help reinforce that desired behavior.

Another tip to remember when teaching friends who may have learning disabilities is to allow plenty of "wait time." Providing wait time means that if you present a question to a friend, allow at least ten seconds for the friend to come up with an answer. You will be amazed at what your friends can come up with when you provide enough processing time! It can seem like a long time to wait, but once you practice it a few times, it becomes more natural.

Mark 6:34 tells us that "When [Jesus] went ashore he saw a great crowd, and he had compassion on them, because they were like sheep without a shepherd. And he began to teach them many things." Throughout the Bible, Jesus teaches us that we are to have compassion on others. The way we respond to the behaviors of our friends is one way to show compassion and be the hands and feet of Jesus.

Encouragement

It is also important to offer encouragement to your students. First Thessalonians 5:11 tells us to "encourage one another, and build one another up, just as you are doing."

Praising and encouraging the individuals in your ministry can set the tone for a positive and happy time together. I have found that when you praise and encourage your friends, they will also begin to praise and encourage each other. What a beautiful thing to see! We are called to share the love of Christ and address challenges with patience and grace.

Encouragement and praise can be given both verbally and nonverbally. Positive affirmation is something that everyone craves from their teachers and leaders. In a paper titled *Positive Greetings at the Door,*[3] Clayton R. Cook says that verbal encouragement can include making behavior-specific praise statements such as, "I love how quietly you are working," simple salutations such as, "Hi! How are you today?" or asking them questions about their week. Nonverbal statements (which can be used often) include giving a high five, thumbs up, fist bump, pat on the back, smile, or side hug. Before engaging in these nonverbal statements, it is a good idea to get a gauge on how comfortable your friend is with physical touch. Some friends prefer no physical contact. For these friends you may consider giving them a sticker or giving them a compliment in front of their parents, caregivers, or peers.

Greeting your friends as they come in the door for Sunday school, a community outreach, or a respite event sets the tone for a great time together. Calling them by name and smiling at their parents or caregivers means so much to the entire family. It helps set the tone for your ministry. Ask if they had a good week at school; and if you have not seen them in a while, you might want to ask their parents or caregivers if there have been any changes recently that you should be aware of to help you serve them better.

As Rudolf Dreikurs once said, " . . . each child needs encouragement like a plant needs water. Without it, his growth is stunted, and his potential is snapped."

Call and Response

"Macaroni and cheese . . . " (says the leader), "Everybody Freeze!" (responds the class). "Everybody in the house" (says the leader),

"Quiet as a mouse!" (responds the class). These are two examples of call and response that I have used in a classroom of young friends. Call-and-response phrases or call-back responses can be used in any ministry setting to get the attention of an entire class. It is wise to practice these phrases before you want to use them so your class knows how to respond when you call out. Call-and-response phrases are usually things that get the attention of the class and tap into their interests so that they enjoy responding. If you have any friends in your class with noise sensitivity, you might consider using a call-and-response phrase that incorporates a calming breathing technique, such as, "Waterfall, waterfall, waterfall . . . " (says the leader), "Shhhhhhhhhh" (responds the class). You can use a call and response when cleaning up or before transitioning to the next activity. The example at the beginning of this paragraph is typically used before a transition or change in activity is about to occur. The purpose of this call and response is to get the attention of the class in a more exciting and engaging way. The second example can be used if your friends are engaged in an activity and they need to become quieter. Call-and-response phrases can be used many times throughout the day as a fun way to get the attention of your class.

Peer Modeling

One of my favorite (and most humbling) stories from my teaching experience involves a boy named Sammy and his friend Lucas. During lunchtime, Sammy liked to eat his dessert first. But one of Sammy's goals at school involved following teacher directions and eating his sandwich first. One day at lunch, Sammy got to his dessert before I could remind him of what to eat first. When I found Sammy in the lunch room, I asked him to put away his dessert and eat his sandwich first. He became upset and fell out of his chair and laid on the floor. I asked him to sit in his seat, but he stayed on the floor. Another teacher walked by and asked him to get back into his seat. He stayed on the floor. Becoming frustrated, I continued to plead with Sammy to sit in his seat. Also becoming frustrated from listening to me repeat myself over and over, Sammy's peer Lucas (in an exhausted tone) said, "Sammy, would you please just get in your seat." Sammy immediately jumped up and got in his seat! It was an eye-opening moment for me that spoke volumes about how useful it can be to use peers in an inclusive environment.

Peer modeling can be used to help your friends of any age learn the routine and rules. A peer model is someone who shows good social behaviors and teaches those skills to others. Peer learning is learning from each other and with each other. Both individuals with and without disabilities can benefit from this modeling and learning style. It can help individuals with and without disabilities form new friendships. And it can help individuals with disabilities gain new skills and reach their goals (as seen in my example).

Using Buddies

Using buddies in your ministry is a wonderful way to implement peer modeling and ensure that all your friends can better participate in the mainstream programs of your church. Buddy ministry provides support to individuals affected by disability with the goal of making church a wonderful experience for everyone involved. A buddy ministry means pairing an individual with a disability with a buddy who does not have a disability during church services or a ministry event.[4] A buddy can be an adult or a peer. Using buddies has been very successful in church programs around the U.S. You will probably want to consider training your buddies in disability etiquette as well as providing them with information about the friend with whom they are going to be serving. Using a buddy could be what helps keep an individual affected by disability in the mainstream classroom.

If you have any friends in your classroom who are tempted to elope (run away), having a buddy system in place can be a wonderful proactive solution. As I have mentioned before, it is good to get as much information from a friend's parents or caregivers as you can, especially if they are prone to eloping. Knowing what does and does not interest your friend can help keep them engaged and can prevent opportunities for running away. Pairing two buddies with this friend can be helpful, providing a second set of eyes to help keep them engaged and safe. As you get to know your friend, you may be able to sense when they are tempted to run and can proactively offer them an opportunity to take a break. If your friend does not seem to enjoy an activity and needs to take a break by going on a walk, the trio can take a walk without any concern of a single buddy being alone with your friend. Having one of your leaders or some of your volunteers positioned near the door can also help prevent your friend from suddenly exiting the room. It can also be a good idea to seat your friend as far from the door of the classroom as possible, making it more difficult for them to elope. When walking around your church facility, it may be helpful to have a buddy holding your friend's hand to keep them engaged rather than focusing on running. You could also consider allowing your friend to help you carry items to wherever you are going. For example, they can help you carry a ball to the gym or cups to the snack area. If these proactive strategies are not effective in preventing your friend from running, you will probably want to consider talking with your church's security team to come up with a more comprehensive safety plan.

As mentioned in the Irresistible Church book *Call Me Friend*, a buddy provides discipleship, friendship, safety, participation, communication assistance, and positive-behavior support. A buddy can also help provide physical assistance for mobility, assist with self-help skills, encourage social interaction, and just be a friend. Buddy ministry can be a great answer to challenges you may face when beginning a disability ministry.

C. *MODIFYING LESSON PLANS*

When leading an inclusive ministry, you may want to consider modifying the lesson plans in order to better meet the needs of all the participants in your classroom. Often, everyone will benefit from the changes, not just your friends with special needs. All individuals are different and have unique learning styles and strengths.

There are many simple modifications you can make for any lesson. However, to do modification well, it will probably take some planning ahead, thinking outside the box, and knowing your class. Of course, you may occasionally have new friends visit your ministry without any warning. If you do not have any information about the visiting individual ahead of time, do as much as you can to make them comfortable and talk to their parents or caregiver if you are able when they drop them off. I have listed a few suggested modifications in this section that will help you make small changes to your directions, your seating, your materials, and your activities.

Directions

The first thing to consider when making changes or modifications in your ministry time is providing directions in small, clear steps. The fewer words you use, the better. When teaching a group of fourth graders a lesson on empathy, I did an activity with them to help them gain a level of understanding of what it might feel like to have a learning disability. I asked for a volunteer, and a young girl bravely stood up. I gave her a long string of directions all at once (stand up, sit down, touch your nose, tap your right foot, etc.). I told her to wait until I was finished with the instructions to perform the tasks I had listed and then said, "OK, go!" The student could not even remember the first step! I asked her how she felt, and she used words such as "overwhelmed," "confused," and "anxious." This is how it can sometimes feel for our friends when we overload them with directions. When I broke down the exercise step by step, the student could do each one and succeeded with confidence. This simple modification when providing directions can make a big difference. If you are able, do not tell the individuals in your class the next step until they have finished the previous one. With a large group, this can be challenging, but it can also be very helpful in helping your class succeed. If your group is too large to move through an activity at the same pace, consider having table leaders or peer buddies who can provide the next step to smaller groups in your class. As I mentioned earlier, using picture cues or other visuals can also be very helpful when teaching individuals with learning disabilities. You could consider modeling the activity in front of the class—a good way to use less talking. Always make sure, however, that as you model an activity, each individual in your class can see you clearly. You can repeat the directions word for word, and then, to ensure that all your friends heard you, have the class repeat the directions after you say them. Before giving any directions, make sure you capture the attention of the class or individual you are addressing. We cannot expect people to follow our directions if they are not aware that we are speaking to them. These are all ways to make modifications in how you give directions, which can set your friends up for success, therefore engaging in more appropriate behaviors.

Seating

Making adaptions to the seating arrangements in your classroom can be a helpful way to keep your friends engaged in the lessons. You might consider placing a student who is easily distracted close to the front or close to the teacher. A leader could lightly tap the shoulder of a student who gets off task, encouraging them to focus again. It can also make an individual feel helpful and important to be seated near the teacher.

Another tip you can consider for the seating arrangements in your classroom is to have flexible seating. You could allow the option of standing during certain activities. This can be very helpful for someone with ADHD who craves movement. You could also provide various seating options such as beanbag chairs, floor pillows, bath mats, yoga balls, or camping chairs. This provides your friends with a choice during your ministry time together. And it can also give them the movement or sensory input that they need to help them focus on the lesson or task.

Materials

Making small changes to the materials you have in your classroom can help your friends succeed. It is a great idea to include large toys for young friends with physical disabilities that present mobility challenges. These can be toys such as large blocks or puzzles with large pieces. For your young friends with cerebral palsy, cause-and-effect toys where you push a button and it sings, moves, or lights up can also be beneficial. Toys that have a lot of interesting textures can be helpful in meeting sensory needs as well. You can glue pegs to puzzle pieces so that a friend with fine motor (hand and finger) challenges can work with the puzzle more easily. Another idea is to cut small pieces of a sponge and glue them to the top of each page of a board book. This allows an individual who cannot easily use their fingers to turn pages in a book the freedom of independently turning pages. You can purchase larger crayons or writing utensils for friends who cannot grasp smaller ones; these can be found at most stores where there is a craft aisle. You might consider using large, colorful pictures for children who have visual impairments.

If you are leading a class of young adults, I encourage you to consider how you can make the lesson and materials match the chronological age of your friends. For example, if you are using photographs, make sure the people in the picture are the same age as your friends. Rereading the story or asking your friends to reread portions of the lesson is a great way to reinforce the materials. I would also suggest leaving time for discussion and questions; allowing your friends the opportunity to verbally process the information will increase their retention as well. Similarly, it can be a great idea to save time for prayer and prayer requests. This provides a powerful and touching opportunity to hear what is going on in the lives of your friends and remind them how important it is to pray. It is also a wonderful way for your friends to build community and use their spiritual gifts by lifting one another up in prayer.

Including visuals and tangible items as you teach your lesson can help individuals with learning impairments grasp a concept more concretely. Being able to touch and hold an item that reinforces the story or lesson can help your friends retain the information. All these ways of adapting your materials help promote independence and confidence in the friends you are teaching. For an example of teaching an age-appropriate lesson to various age groups, check out the online appendices for this book.

Activities

When designing the activities for your Sunday morning ministry, a respite event, or community outreach, there are a few things that can be helpful to keep in mind regarding activities. It can be very beneficial for people of all abilities to do hands-on activities instead of worksheets. People of all ages and learning styles typically like to use their hands and can usually retain more information when doing so. If an individual has difficulty using their hands or is sensitive to certain textures, you can allow them to use your hands. You would do this by placing your hands *under* their hands. With their hand on top of yours, they can feel what you are doing as you hold or manipulate an item. You can also place your hand on top of your friend's hand, helping them with whatever the activity is by gently leading their hand through it. If a friend has motor-skill difficulties, especially fine motor, you can pre-cut or arrange things ahead of time. This can take a bit more work planning and preparing, but it could make a huge difference in the flow of your lesson. You might also consider engaging volunteers just for this who are willing to help with some of the prep work. If an individual has fine-motor challenges, you can also place his or her paper on a nonslip pad to keep their paper from falling off the table or moving around.

PART IV

Conclusion

All behavior is communication. When we are presented with challenging behaviors in our ministries, we have the opportunity to be the hands and feet of Jesus by responding with compassion and finding the intended meaning behind that behavior. Matthew 25:34-40 reminds us that when we serve others in need, we are serving the Lord. By understanding behavior as communication and putting a little thought into our proactive strategies, we can better serve the families that come to us. With an open heart, open mind, and the willingness to do things a bit differently, we can more effectively meet their needs. We can provide families affected by disability with a wonderful and welcoming experience when they enter the doors of our church or ministry. We can become an Irresistible Church that compels people with disabilities to fully belong. As I think about families who are impacted by disabilities that result in challenging behaviors, I truly feel that they are the ones who need a welcoming church more than anyone. Parents and caregivers need respite and fellowship, siblings need to meet new friends their age and have discipleship opportunities, our friends with disabilities need to feel the comfort of a safe place and new friends, and the whole family needs to feel the love of Jesus. I hope that after reading this book you believe me when I say, "You, my friend, can make this happen!"

Notes

1. http://www.autism-community.com/communication/communication-and-behavior
2. https://www.education.com/reference/article/visual-schedule-classroom-autism-ASD
3. www.sjoe.org/selpararesources/toers/Positive_Greetings_at_the_Door_script.doc.pdf
4. *Call Me Friend*, 2016, p. 7.

Becoming *Irresistible*

Luke 14 commands Christ followers to "Go quickly . . . find the blind, the lame, and the crippled . . . and compel them to come in!" While this sounds inspiring and daunting, exciting and overwhelming, motivating and frightening, all at the same time, what does it actually mean? How do we live and function within the church in such a way that families affected by disability are compelled to walk through our doors to experience the body of Christ?

We can certainly *compel* them by offering programs, ministries, events, and other church activities, but what if the compelling aspect was more about heart, culture, acceptance and embracing? What if our churches were overflowing with the hope of Jesus Christ . . . a hope not simply for those who "fit in" or look the part, but rather a hope to all, including the marginalized, downtrodden and outcast?

Becoming *Irresistible* is more than programs and activities–it is about a transformational work in our hearts . . . first as individuals and then as the body of Christ. *Irresistible* allows us to see each individual as he or she truly is: created in the image of God (Genesis 1:26-27), designed purposely as a masterpiece (Psalm 139:13-14), instilled with purpose, plans and dreams (Jeremiah 29:11), and a truly indispensable member of the kingdom of God (1 Corinthians 12:23). An *Irresistible Church* is an "authentic community built on the hope of Christ that compels people affected by disability to fully belong." It is powerful for a person to know that he or she is fully welcomed and belongs. *Irresistible* captures the heart of the church as it should be—how else do we explain the rapid growth and intense attraction to the church in the book of Acts? The heart of God was embodied through the people of God by the Spirit of God . . . and that is simply *Irresistible*!

The Irresistible Church Series is designed to help not only shape and transform the heart of the church, but also to provide the practical steps and activities to put *flesh* around the *heart* of the church—to help your church become a place for people to fully belong. Thank you for responding to the call to become *Irresistible*. It will not happen overnight, but it will happen. As with all good things, it requires patience and perseverance, determination and dedication, and ultimately an underlying trust in the faithfulness of God. May God bless you on this journey. Be assured that you are not alone—there are many on the path of *Irresistible*.

For more information or to join the community,
please visit www.irresistiblechurch.org.

Joni and Friends was established in 1979 by Joni Eareckson Tada, who at 17 was injured in a diving accident, leaving her a quadriplegic. Since its inception, Joni and Friends has been dedicated to extending the love and message of Christ to people who are affected by disability whether it is the disabled person, a family member, or friend. Our objective is to meet the physical, emotional, and spiritual needs of this group of people in practical ways.

Joni and Friends is committed to recruiting, training, and motivating new generations of people with disabilities to become leaders in their churches and communities. Today, the Joni and Friends International Disability Center serves as the administrative hub for an array of programs which provide outreach to thousands of families affected by disability around the globe. These include two radio programs, an award-winning television series, the Wheels for the World international wheelchair distribution ministry, Family Retreats which provide respite for those with disabilities and their families, Field Services to provide church training along with educational and inspirational resources at a local level, and the Christian Institute on Disability to establish a firm biblical worldview on disability-related issues.

From local neighborhoods to the far reaches of the world, Joni and Friends is striving to demonstrate to people affected by disability, in tangible ways, that God has not abandoned them—he is with them—providing love, hope, and eternal salvation.

Available Now in the Irresistible Church Series

Start with Hello

Introducing Your Church to Special Needs Ministry

Families with special needs often share that they desire two things in their church: accessibility and acceptance. Accessibility to existing structures, programs and people is an imperative. Acceptance with a sense of belonging by the others who also participate in the structures, programs and fellowship of the church is equally necessary. In this simple book you'll learn the five steps to becoming an accessible and accepting church.

To receive first notice of upcoming resources, including respite, inclusive worship and support groups, please contact us at churchrelations@joniandfriends.org.

Other Recommended Resources

Beyond Suffering Bible

The *Beyond Suffering Bible* by Joni and Friends is the first study Bible made specifically for those who suffer and the people who love them. Uplifting insights from Joni Eareckson Tada and numerous experts and scholars who have experienced suffering in their own lives and will help you move beyond the "why" of suffering to grasp the eternal value God is building into our lives. Special features include: inspiring devotionals, biblical and contemporary profiles, Bible reading plans, connection points and disability ministry resources.

Find out more at http://www.joniandfriends.org/store/category/bibles/

Beyond Suffering® Student Edition

Beyond Suffering for the Next Generation: A Christian View on Disability Ministry will equip young people to consider the issues that affect people with disabilities and their families, and inspire them to action. Students who embrace this study will gain confidence to join a growing, worldwide movement that God is orchestrating to fulfill Luke 14:21-23: "Go out quickly into the streets and alleys of the town and bring in the poor, the crippled, the blind, and the lame.... so that my house will be full."

ISBN: 978-0-9838484-6-2
304 pages · 8.5″ x 11″
Includes CD-ROM

Joni: An Unforgettable Story

In this unforgettable autobiography, Joni reveals each step of her struggle to accept her disability and discover the meaning of her life. The hard-earned truths she discovers and the special ways God reveals his love are testimonies to faith's triumph over hardship and suffering. This new edition includes an afterword, in which Joni talks about the events that have occurred in her life since the book's original publication in 1976, including her marriage and the expansion of her worldwide ministry to families affected by disability.

ISBN: 978-0310240013
205 pages · Paperback

www.joniandfriends.org · P.O. Box 3333, Agoura Hills, CA 91376
(818) 707-5664 · Fax: (818) 707-2391 TTY: (818) 707-9707

Customizable Resources from the Book

Available for Download at

http://www.irresistiblechurch.org/library

Joni and Friends

THE IRRESISTIBLE CHURCH

Basic Parent Interview Form

This simple form can be used to collect information about your friends, allowing you to better serve them during your ministry time.

Help us to know all you would like us to know about your child!

Child's Name: ______________ DOB: ______________

Parent's Name: ______________

Siblings and ages: ______________

Does your child have a disability? ______________

If so, please tell us about it? ______________

Please list any safety concerns: ______________

Your child's favorite things

Color: ______________ Books: ______________

Toys: ______________ Other favorite things: ______________

What are some things your child does NOT enjoy?

What are your goals for your child at church?

Any other things you would like for us to know about your child or family.

Joni and Friends • The Irresistible Church Series • Call and Response Phrases • http://www.irresistiblechurch.org

Basic Parent Interview Form

Joni and Friends

THE IRRESISTIBLE CHURCH

Call and Response Phrases

Call and response phrases can be used to capture the attention of a classroom or group of people. Practicing these ahead of when you use them will help make them more effective.

Leader says...	Class response...
"Macaroni and cheese"	"Everybody freeze"
"Everybody in the house"	"Quiet as a mouse"
"I'm in the Lord's army"	"Yes sir"
"Waterfall, waterfall, waterfall"	Shhhhhhhhhhh"
"All Set"	"You bet"
"Jesus loves me"	"This I know"
"Who loves you"	"You do"
"1,2,3 Eyes on Me"	"1,2 Eyes on you"

Joni and Friends • The Irresistible Church Series • Call and Respo

Call and Response Phrases

Joni and Friends

THE IRRESISTIBLE CHURCH

Teaching the Concept of Salvation

The concept of Salvation is one that should be taught to every age group and level. However, *how* you teach it may look very different depending on your Below you will find a few ways of presenting this lesson that will appeal to v groups.

Lesson Passage: Romans 10:9-10 - "because, if you confess with your mo Jesus is Lord and believe in your heart that God raised him form the dead, y saved. For with the heart one believes and is justified, and with the mouth confesses and is saved."

Tips for Teaching Preschoolers:

- Use simple wording
- Incorporate movement
- Teach a song with motions
- Use visual pictures
- Make Gospel bracelets
- Use repetition to help your friends remember the key points

Tips for Teaching Elementary Schoolers:

- Have them to draw it out
  - Use blank paper or coloring sheets
  - Encourage them to share their drawings with a peer
- Use the *Wordless Book*
  - This tool uses blocks or pages of color to represent the Gospel truths
  - http://www.berean.org/bibleteacher/wbpage.html
- Use online videos or YouTube
  - Saddleback kids has free online videos
- Use tangible items – ex. A giant heart cutout when talking about God's love
- Teach the ABCs of becoming a Christian
  - Admit, Believe, Confess

Friends • The Irresistible Church Series • Call and Response Phrases • http://www.irresistiblechurch.org

Teaching the Concept of Salvation

Joni and Friends
INTERNATIONAL DISABILITY CENTER